My Story: Journey to Purpose

Paul A. Blake

Copyright

ISBN-978-976-95942-6-5

Cover design by Andrew Blake

Published by Words Worthit Publishers

Available on Amazon Kindle and online stores

Dedication

I dedicate this book to my parents, Brenton Blake, and Joan Hynes, whose love and nurturing has enabled me to strive for greatness. They are far from perfect, but they are the parents that God gifted me with, fulfilling my purpose. Your commitment to your own dreams after investing in your children's lives and education is remarkable. The difficult things that you had to endure did not stop your sacrifice for us. My love for you both is more than words can express; if I had to live another lifetime, I would still choose you to be my parents. This book is for you both to understand how your commitment to raising me has taken me from Journey to Purpose.

Introduction

How our lives will turn out is anybody's guess. There are things we can control, while others we can't. Whatever the case, how we decide to play our lot in life will make the difference. I was a victim, but today, I choose to live life as a victor over my circumstances. I hope in writing these words, someone will read them and take a different direction in life. My story is not just my story. It is the story of every person in the world told they could not be great. It is a story of how simple words of encouragement can change destructive behaviours and set us on a path of finding success and abundance. I want the world to know that nobody needs to resign to living a life of defeat when the world has so much to offer us.

Writing my story has brought out many emotions in me. I did not want to share things with the world, but like Jeremiah, the prophet, I cannot but to speak because my soul is burning, and I cannot help it. Writing these words, I have felt anger, sadness, excitement, regret, frustration, gratitude, humility and other feelings that I can't explain. Still, I am thankful because they have helped to make this possible. I want someone to read my words and understand that nothing in this world is strong enough to keep them down if they have the will to fight. They may lose some battles, but they must win the war if the Lord is on their side.

I present my story as a gift to anyone passionate about finding their purpose and living an abundant life. It is not another self-help book that promises to give you the keys to unlock the fountain of youth. It is a book that as you read and turn the pages, you will receive insight into my struggles, failures, and triumphs. Understand that I am a fighter, life struck down many times, but each time I have gotten up to live to fight another day. I want my story to change lives; I want someone to know that nothing in this world can hold them back if they decide to soar to greatness despite their circumstances.

TABLE OF CONTENTS

The opportunity to share my journey with the world is a wonderful privilege. I hope my story will help someone find his or her purpose amid the negative pronouncements of those without vision. Those who have had failures and heartaches don't believe they are here to do something spectacular. My story is not unique, but it is my story, and I will tell it as it is. I want no special recognition or accolades. If my journey helps to shape the life of one individual who desires to live an abundant life, I will be happy to die knowing I have contributed.

My story began on September 4, 1973, in the parish of Manchester. My parents, Brenton and Joan Hynes (Blake) got married at the tender age of 19 and 18, respectively, after finding out my mother was pregnant while in college. I spend much of my childhood in the town of Mandeville, living in several places. Things were not bad, but they were also not very good. I am convinced that my parents should never have gotten married. At this point in life, I believe that the best thing they did for us (children) was getting divorced, though it did not feel that way (that's for another part of the journey).

I think I had a regular life up to age nine. Although mom and dad did not always get along; we had some fun times. Looking back through all the pain and hurt, I realise that they too were products of a dysfunctional cycle. They related to each other and their children out of a misinformed position, thinking they were the best parents. All the quarrels and the fights were things that they would have learned from observing their dysfunctional parents and grandparents before them. I understand and empathize with this kind of dysfunction because of studying counselling and psychology. I no longer blame them for their shortcomings, as a matter of fact; because of them, I know the true meaning of forgiveness.

I am no longer afraid of my truth. Too often, we strive to preserve images that add more problems to healing than the solutions provided. Today, I can say with pride that my parents, with all their flaws, have been the ones from whom I have learned some of the most important lessons. One of those lessons is that parents are not perfect; they do what they do with what they have been given. Sometimes it works, but at other times it doesn't, and the most that anyone can pray for is that in the mix knowledge is gained that will aid in making better decisions.

"We all have to begin somewhere, good, the outcome is determined by our desire to see it through to the end".

I am not an authority on any subject, nor am I an expert on the best way to get the most out of life. What I do know is that life is a journey and success is hard. I was never an A student, as a matter of fact, academically, school for me was less than attractive. It took me repeating grade eleven to obtain six subjects, and even then, my passes were average. Though I enjoyed going to school, it was not for academic exploits. I enjoyed school because I had a gang of friends who knew what it meant to enjoy life, even when we had people telling us we were going nowhere in life. Reflecting on these several years later, I have concluded that I was no dunce; it's just that I was not too fond of what was being taught.

Hardship was my best friend in high school. I went through things that only a few people are privy to, and I thank God above every day for these people who helped me maintain my sanity (Metro, Audy, Wayne, Eshaun, Simone, Leset and Sherlyn). These people, along with a few others, gave me a lifeline in more ways than one. School can be a cruel place when dealing with people who cannot appreciate others' experiences because of their sheltered lives. I have had to forgive a few people, as I now understand that their actions were out of ignorance.

The pain of dealing with parents getting divorced was psychologically and emotionally toxic and affects children's life in unusual ways. Such was my life at the beginning of my third year (third form). Sometimes it's difficult to understand how I made it through those years, but thank God I did. Everything began going downhill in September 1988, and it was only a matter of what else could go wrong that kept the clock ticking. This was also the year of Hurricane Gilbert, so one can imagine the turmoil of having your life turned upside down by things outside of your control. It is not a good feeling.

"If you continue to believe you can't fly, you will never find a reason to grow wings".

The search for identity can be a steep road to travel. I look back at my younger years and compare them to the person I am now and realise that I knew little about myself. Growing up in an environment often filled with negative conversations can affect how children view the world. The influence of my mother saved me in more ways than one. When people said I was no good and destined to live a life of failure; she told me I was born to be great. Even when I was unsure of my ability, this was the one thought that kept me pushing forward to discover my purpose.

However, the struggles were real. My most significant battle was to believe that I was worthy of being among the best. Growing up poor has a way of painting a picture in our minds that we will never measure up to others, and in my mind, I did not measure up. Because of this, I often hid in the shadows just so that I would not be noticed, hoping that none would find out how much I was in poverty. Today I realise I suffered more from the mind's misery than I was suffering from physical poverty. My situation was not unique. I have discovered that many people cannot achieve greatness because this mentality still imprisons them.

I struggled with not understanding why the world was so unfair to some, yet treated others with so much favour. No one could have prepared me for a life of growing up in an environment where I was regularly put down. My parents had fallen on hard times, which resulted in us having to go back to the country to live. I struggled to make sense of my circumstances, so I frequently asked if we had done something wrong and were now paying the price. Being a child, I never really understood much of what was happening. Still, years later, it would begin to make sense because of new information and insight into how behaviours can change when people think you have disappointed them.

Through it all, I have learned that some of the most challenging situations will help prepare us for more extraordinary things. Had it not been for my struggles, I would not have discovered the real measure of my strength. I now have a positive attitude towards life and look at every obstacle I must overcome. Struggles teach us valuable lessons, and I am learning that success is about making the right choices no matter what your battles are.

"Your struggles are the building blocks of your future success".

A lesson I have learned on my journey to becoming successful is dealing with disappointments. In my search to discover my passion and purpose, I came across many people who at first shared the excitement and joy that I felt. Mostly, many of these individuals are genuine people. Still, for whatever reasons, promises of follow-up meetings, access to much-needed resources or networking rarely materialized. When this happens, our first inclination is to drown ourselves in disappointment. I now know this is the worst thing I can do in fulfilling my mission.

Being disappointed in people's inability to deliver on promises and expectations will not help us get to where we need to be. I have wasted too much energy being angry and disappointed when people I depend on don't deliver. I often lose sight that I can find a way to do what I had asked for or needed done. Though feelings of disappointment are a natural reaction to unfulfilled promises, I can choose not to allow it to define my success. Approximately 90 percent of what we expect people to do or deliver on for us will end in disappointment. That leaves a mere 10 percent to work with. So what are the odds of us never being disappointed?

I am responsible for my success. I hope and pray that I will get some much-needed help along the way, but I will not allow it to shape my destiny if it does not happen. Yes, I will be disappointed because I am only human, but there is so much more to life than what people don't deliver on. Every time someone disappoints me because of some undelivered promise or unmet expectation, I will look at it as an opportunity to learn how to equip myself for future success.

"Disappointments are often disguised opportunities waiting to be unwrapped."

To say I've come a long way is putting it mildly. There were times I did not think I would make it. When life throws many curve balls at you, the most natural thing to do is give up trying. I have had my fair share of trials and bittersweet moments when I felt like there was no further down, I could have gone. I know what it is like to make plans for success and to set things in motion only to watch them fall apart. I know what it is like to be disappointed by friends and family. I had made excuses when I did not follow through on things I should. I know how to play the blame game when I come up short of fulfilling a promise made, whether to myself or others. Despite all the challenges, the most important lesson I have learned is never to give up, regardless of how circumstances look or how I may feel. Life is never about my failures or disappointments. Instead, I will make the best of every situation and my commitment to finding my purpose in this world.

I am unsure sometimes of the impact I am making in the lives of people I meet. I often wonder if my ambitions are unrealistic; I worry about getting ahead of myself in pursuing my dreams. I sometimes doubt my abilities and need to hear kind words of assurance from a friend, family member, or colleague. When this happens, it reminds me of how much I am only human. Even though I sometimes feel this way, I try not to dwell in that state for very long. There is a fire burning in my soul that can only be quenched when I discover my purpose and pursue it with passion. I am committed to living a life of purpose, or I will die trying. Life is too short not to live it on my terms; I refuse to give up until my life's mission is achieved.

I don't know where life will take me, but I am determined to find out. I am convinced that the best is yet to come, and I am not giving up until I have found the best of me. I am inspired to take on the challenges of living life, knowing that I am here to make a difference. I am here to change the world, and nothing will stop me from leaving my footprints in the sands of time.

There is so much I am yet to accomplish, and there is no time to waste. I will not dwell on yesterday's disappointments and failures because today is a new day. My inspiration comes from knowing that I am proof that those who don't give up will beat the odds and eventually enjoy the fruits of their labour.

"A steady diet of positive things will inspire, your soul to reach its full potential".

The price of success is understanding that, though you may not see how your circumstances relate to the future, you continue to pursue your dreams. It is not over until the last trumpet sounds. I have fought many battles in my life; some I have won, others I have had to leave the field battered and wounded. However, the tune that keeps playing in my head is that there is still another mile I must walk when I think I am at the end of the road. I have learned that it is never over because I am still here, drawing breath from a life of possibilities.

I have found myself at a crossroads before, not knowing which direction to turn. I have given up and drown in my self-pity; likewise, I have blamed others for not being able to pursue my dreams. The only place this has ever taken me is on the highway to nowhere. I have had to learn the painful lesson of taking responsibility for my actions and living with the consequences. I know it's not over because, despite my many failures, I have the tremendous privilege of telling a great story. I know it's not over because there is something worth adding to the wellspring of life each day.

The only way it will be over is when I give in to defeat, but I was not called to live a defeated life. I am a child of purpose put on this earth to carve out my name in history. Because my story is not complete, I can never say that it is over. Every day is a new opportunity to become my best self. I may not get it right all the time, but until then, I commit to keeping on trying because there is so much I need to accomplish. It is not over until I can do no more of what I was called to do.

When you finally discover what you are capable of doing, it is hard to accept anything but giving your best".

As much as we desire success, the fear of succeeding beyond expectations is something we often struggle with. When we accomplish great things, we sometimes don't think that we are worthy of them because we have listened to the negative around us for so long. This is how I used to feel. Still, I am learning each day to overcome these feelings by reminding myself that I am gifted and purpose-driven as the people who are my role models. When we give in to fear, nobody wins. The world would have lost the chance to witness something special, and we would have missed the opportunity to take our rightful place in the world.

I am not saying that I am entirely without fear because a little of it serves its purpose to remind us we are only human. However, I do not subscribe to having fear rule over me so I cannot maximize my potential. When people around me try to make me feel I cannot do great things, I will push through because I have absolutely nothing to lose. I have nothing to fear because I am in control of my destiny. The things I cannot control are not worth worrying about.

Fear is a thing of the past; I did not believe in the power of my purpose. Today, even though I get apprehensive when I am being stretched to the limit of my potential, I will go out and conquer the world. Fear is a matter of what we allow to imprison our minds, so the best thing that any of us can do is free our minds from the negative stuff that fills the air. I no longer fear being successful at anything I set my sights on. I too have a right to claim my place in this magnificent home called the universe.

"Living in fear is not an investment; it's an expensive liability".

It is an extraordinary privilege to be alive for such a time as this. So much to give God thanks for despite the struggles and numerous trials. I am in awe each time I reflect on the journey it has taken to now stand in the place where I can positively influence people's lives. God is awesome. I did not do anything to deserve all the blessings that have been poured out in my life, but He saw it fit to extend His grace and mercy and count me worthy of His calling.

There is so much more left to be accomplished, and though at times the path seems unclear, I have learnt to depend on the Lord's guiding, and He has never failed me. I am willing to follow where He leads, for I am confident that all things will work out for my benefit and His glory. I am genuinely excited about the next stage of this journey that I fully plan to embrace with passion and purpose.

Like a fine wine, 44 is indeed a good year. I may be a year older, but I am also a lot wiser and more prepared to take on life. I greet each day with the expectation of impacting the lives of those around me. Sometimes the way I expect life to go does not quite work that way, but who am I to question the master's plan? In all things, I have learned to give thanks and to take nothing for granted. I try to complain less because it changes very little. What I have committed to doing instead is to look for opportunities within each circumstance. Forty-four is indeed a great year, but I will not stop now. The journey has just begun.

"Never doubt the potential that you possess. Stop listening to people who can't recognise you for what you are worth".

When life takes an unexpected path and circumstances don't always work out for the best, it is easy to start thinking that it is your destiny to live defeated. It takes courage to step out of the shadows and claim the success for which you were designed. Such has been my journey on this long and challenging road to discovering my purpose. It is not easy to begin believing in how much potential and power you have within you when the people you allow in your space discourage you the most. However, if you want to taste success, you must be courageous enough to take on life, even if it means doing it alone.

It requires courage to tune out the negative voices around you and move on to something more significant. When I was younger, I listened to what others had to say about me, and sometimes this caused me to cower in fear, often refusing to believe in my God-given abilities. I allowed people to dictate the terms of my participation in life because I thought I was not brilliant enough, vibrant enough, or worthy enough. However, once I discovered there was much more to living than being among the status quo, life took on new meaning.

Having courage does not mean that your life will be absent of moments of self-doubt or times when you want to resign to just being counted among the living. What it means is being brave enough to accept your shortcomings and boldly step into your purpose. It demands that you stop measuring yourself against others' standards and find comfort in knowing that you are always doing your best. I have committed to being courageous. I will not be afraid of life, even if it does not work the way I envision it. Life is too short not to live it to the fullest!

Courage is not about being unafraid of obstacles in your way. Courage is about taking life's obstacles and using them to your benefit despite the odds".

My journey has been one of many pieces, which sometimes did not seem to relate to each other. Sometimes the pieces drifted so far apart that I thought I would not have made it. However, those pieces of our lives serve a higher purpose; they are there to keep us grounded in truth and help us walk a straight path. Putting back the pieces means having the courage to take on life, even after facing disappointments and heartaches. Please don't be ashamed of your pieces because they are as much a part of who you are as the air you breathe.

I have been pulled apart by life so often. It is difficult to remember the details of the varying circumstances I encountered. Sometimes I handled the situation with the grace of a swan. At other times I crashed like Humpty Dumpty hitting the ground at maximum speed. When I collapsed, I learned some of the most important lessons that I still find very useful. When the pieces were drifting out of place, I discovered that I am more resilient than I thought. When the fragments were out of place, I found the strength to give life one more try.

No matter how messed up life gets, the opportunity for putting back together the pieces is always available to us. The fact is, we just can't stop trying. Life will beat us up, throw us down and kick us where it hurts most, but it does not have to defeat us. When the pieces are out of place, take the time to step back and rearrange them until you get that perfect picture.

"You are here at this moment because it was never in God's intention for you to remain a broken vessel".

It is easy to believe that you are the recipient of a hard knock life because of circumstances. When it seems like life is just one awful experience after another, hope is often as elusive as the pot of gold at the end of the rainbow. What makes matters worse is being in the presence of people who would prefer to see you fail, rather than uplifting you. Often, they do this because somehow your potential for being successful is a threat to their existence. In all of this, the key is to never give up on life; things are not always what they appear to be.

On my journey to success, I have learned to trust those things that remain constant. Even when I feel like giving up. If I pay attention to the negative stuff, I will lose sight of what is truly meaningful. In my early years, I allowed what others had to say about my circumstances to dictate the choices I made and what I wanted people to think of me. I kept myself in a box by believing the lies of those who appeared better off than me, not understanding that I was born to serve a higher purpose. I have learned that people who do not mean you will work overtime to keep you where they can always exploit your flaws.

However, life is not always what it appears to be. You may be the product of the worst kind of circumstance, but it does not mean that you must allow it to shape your destiny. If you continue to wallow in self-pity because of where you come from or the opportunities you were not afforded; eventually, you will feel quite comfortable living among the swine. Learn how to look beyond what you are going through and discover your purpose for being alive. I found my reason for being on this earth. To make a difference in the lives of those who need hope. My circumstances do not define me because I have conquered all the hurdles.

"If you are unhappy with your present life, think about changing your attitude towards living".

Here I am again, reflecting on the things that have helped to shape the person I am today. Though high school holds many memories that I would not trade for anything, there are some things I am not eager to remember. When you come from humble circumstances, associating with children of different social backgrounds, inexperience and ignorance can cause children to be cruel and insensitive in their treatment of others. When I recall the times, they treated me or others with unkindness; it is with a sense of forgiveness, because I now understand that we are products of our environment.

Most of the people I went to school with are worth remembering. People who would give a portion of their meal or split their lunch money so those of us who were not so privileged would not endure attending classes bearing the pains of hunger. Some students could not relate to the fact that a few of us came to school without necessities, not because we wanted to, but because our parents could not afford it. Our parents sent us to school without these things because they wanted a much better life for us than they had.

Today, I have learned to forgive people in my circle. I forgive, not for their sake, but for my own. Being teased and ridiculed because I could not afford necessities to survive daily was damaging psychologically. It was even more impactful within the school environment. There are several incidents I can remember where because I did not have lunch or had to borrow money from someone. It turned into an embarrassing situation.

I can vividly recall one incident when a youngster openly discussed how my parents were cruffish (bums) because I had no money for lunch. He said this not knowing that morning my mother had divided her taxi fare amongst three of us to get to school, while she walked half of the journey.

Another incident I recall was when a classmate said he would rather throw half his lunch into the garbage than let me have it. That day I passed an exam with my stomach growling like a hungry bear awaken from hibernation.

Even though I sometimes feel the pain when I look back at these things, it does not make me bitter. I have learned that the best medicine for a hurting heart is forgiveness. I can reminisce with many of the persons with whom I had little in common with back then, feeling at ease and comfortable in my skin. I would not trade the unpleasant experiences for better ones because they helped me view life differently and appreciate any situation's simplicity. The people who ridiculed me did not break me; they were preparing me for greater things.

"Looking back does not mean staying in the past. It means using the history of the experiences as a catalyst for a brighter future."

The difference between success and failure sometimes depends on the support system that is available to you. No matter how hard you try, you will realise that you cannot do it alone one day. It's a valuable lesson I have had to learn over time, and I am still learning. Even when I don't think I need people's help to complete my journey, something happens that reminds me of how much I need others' support. It is not the easiest of lessons to learn. Still, it is worth learning to save you from unnecessary frustration and heartache.

Our support systems are not necessarily permanent fixtures in our lives. Some people will be with us for the long haul, while others will only be available for a season. I've had to come to terms with this and realise that when people disappoint me; they are a part of my journey up to that point. Therefore, I will need others to become a part of my support system to take me the rest of the journey. Another lesson I have learned is not to be attached to any support system that when it goes away, my entire life comes crashing down with it. Though I need my support system, it is not the sole reason for my existence. What I need to do is learn how to use it to my advantage.

Choose your support system wisely; whether you believe it, not everyone is right for you. Even people with good intentions can be toxic, sometimes even unconsciously. I learn that the people I need to support me are the ones that value my efforts. They will share my vision and will be there to help me through my success or failure. A healthy support system is not only to know the right people. It is networking with the people who will mutually benefit you, as much as you do them. My support system is built on the principle of each one helping the other one until the journey is complete.

"The people in your life will either push you towards your purpose or be the silent killers of your dreams; so choose your friends wisely".

In this life, you need an attitude that is defined by a mission to succeed. People who desire to lead productive lives, find their passion and fulfill their purpose will not receive any favours. You will have to struggle to overcome those individuals who will try to point out that the vision you have for yourself is unrealistic. Such persons will do everything in their power to keep you confined to the small space they have created for you. If they can't have their way, they will work assiduously to kill your dreams or get you to doubt your God-given abilities. It requires a purposeful spirit to elevate yourself above this kind of distraction and pursue the life of purpose for which you were created. Finding purpose is what will make the difference between being victorious or resigning in defeat.

On this journey towards self-actualization, my purpose has not always been clear. I've had to struggle with inadequacy feelings that subdued me for a significant portion of my life. It is easy to believe the lies of people who don't mean you well if you don't have a good idea of who you are. It took me deliberately adjusting my thought process and seeing life from a new perspective to understand that I am here to accomplish great things. I am now more committed to seeing my limitations as opportunities for growth rather than obstacles. I was meant to live a purpose-driven life, and I will not stop until I achieve it.

I am working on finding my purpose daily because unimportant stuff has lost their appeal. I am not overly concerned about being rich or famous; I desire to discover the joy of living an abundant life.

I refuse to lie down and die even when the odds are against me because how then would I appreciate the joy of what could have been. I will be passionate about the life I have lived with my last breath because the journey has been worth it. The road may have been challenging, but on it, I found out what it means to celebrate life. It is not the money, fame or fortune that makes this life worth living. It is discovering your purpose for being here and passionately pursuing it with all your might.

"When you begin to walk in your purpose, you complain less about life's minor setbacks".

As I contemplate the next phase of my life, I cannot help but recall several aspects of my brief life. Most of it is wonderful memories that I will always cherish, while there are other parts I would prefer to forget. Still, I would never be the person I am today without these things being a part of my journey. Life is a series of transitions, and whether or not we like it, it is worth remembering that the decision is made regarding which road we must take. Recalling the negative stuff that has happened may bring about pain and cause reservations. Still, there are lessons to learn that can help us make better decisions as we write our success story. Anything worth remembering is worth learning from. There is hardly a memory that does not have a vital lesson that will help us understand the measure of our strength.

What are the things that I remember? I remember being told I would not amount to much I believed this lie. I remember being called a failure because I did not dance to the tune that others played. Even when opposed, I dance to my beat because I knew nothing was wrong with the song I was playing. The problem was often with those listening. I shared my dreams of becoming an author and motivational speaker with someone who was supposed to be my friend and was encouraged to do something more realistic. He explained with sincerity that many persons who did this failed, and he was afraid I would end up among the statistics. I listened to what this person had to say about me, but I refused to pursue my passion for writing and public speaking because of fear. I have been told I was not good looking, tall or muscular or popular enough to hang out in some circles. I have been told that I don't have the qualities it takes to be a successful motivational speaker. Life is not so much about remembering the stuff that was said or done to you, but more about overcoming the negative perceptions and charting your destiny.

Fast forward 20 years. Today, I have begun to live my dream, and I do so without apology or asking anyone's permission. I have finally discovered my purpose, and I am passionately fulfilling my destiny. The scars are still there, but I have been able to use those years of negative pronouncements as a catalyst to propel me into the path of greatness. I cannot afford to be fearful of the unknown; I must do what I can while I have the strength to do it. Yes, sometimes I still remember the cruel jokes at my expense, but it is no longer with a sense of bitterness. One of the valuable lessons I have learnt from this is that victory arises from the ashes of perseverance. Another lesson is that when people in your space don't understand your journey, they can only act in ignorance, which breeds contempt.

 It's why it is crucial to learn to have a heart of forgiveness towards who has hurt you. For all the pain and anguish I must endure, I have learnt that life rewards those who refuse to give up. This is my story.

"Embrace your past, live in the present, and look to the future with high expectations".

Most of the outcomes of life have to do with the decisions that we make. Sometimes decisions are easy to make, and the rewards are lasting, but at other times, making them can be so difficult, they will rock your world. As I write my story, I reflect on the many choices I have had to make in my life. I've not always made the best decisions, but I can say that each one has helped shape the person I am in one way or another. As I journey through life, I will not fear the choices that are ahead because they are a part of my journey towards greatness. Each decision will become a page of the fantastic story that I will need to tell the world. There is nothing in me to fear but fear itself, so whatever decisions I make, I am willing to stand by them.

With that said, I believe the most fulfilling decision I have made to date is to pursue my dream of becoming a published author and motivational speaker. It has not been an easy feat, mainly because I have often doubted my abilities, and some were more than willing to assist me in believing that. I had to learn that my desire to find my purpose was in my determination to rise above my detractors. Life is about taking chances, and one day I woke up and decided to take a leap of faith and step into my purpose. Whatever the odds are, everyone will eventually have to choose to sink or swim when they are tossed in the deep end of the pool. I decided it was better to swim.

I want to use my journey to encourage others who are afraid of making that bold step into greatness. When I pursued my passion, I did not know where the path would lead, but I am happy that I was brave enough to find and follow it. Decisions often will take us out of our comfort zones and will test the strength of our metal. One thing is sure; deciding to chase your dreams pays enormous dividends, even if you must suffer several setbacks. I resolved to step out of the shadows of doubt and fear and spread my wings and soar. Life will always be about decisions, and if you don't decide about your life, it will decide for you.

"If you invest heavily in the counsel of fools, don't expect anything more than what you have spent".

I never imagined I would know what success would feel like. I had a false idea of what successful living was because of my upbringing for most of my life. Success for me meant to access all the things that I never had the privilege of enjoying. My idea of success was to be able to afford multiple pairs of shoes. It meant having enough clothes to choose from daily and being able to buy that fancy house or luxury car or just having enough to eat. The things that many people took for granted became my marker for a successful life. Only those who grew up in similar circumstances can relate to what I am talking about.

Fast forward twenty-five years, my idea of success has been altered tremendously. I now know that I have been successful in several areas of my life, which I did not consider important before. One of these areas has to do with me discovering my purpose and passionately pursuing it. It is like learning the value of breathing again. I love being able to speak words of empowerment into souls that have not yet discovered the greatness within them. Through finding my purpose, I have come to understand that life is not about what you receive, but more about what you give, which will be returned to you in ways you cannot imagine.

My success is about living the abundant life, a life that understands people's real value and the gifts they deposit for a time on this earth. It is about living a changed life where my failures do not restrict me because of what others think. Success for me is to feel comfortable in my skin and not being a people pleaser. I am successful because I live to serve others. I will not allow myself to feel bad because of what I don't have; I would rather spend my precious time celebrating the joy of being alive at this moment. Success for me is learning to view the glass as always half full and commit to having it full eventually.

"The chances of you being successful are magnified when your attitude is in the right place".

Life is not perfect, and neither are our families. I can genuinely say mine is as far from perfection as the north is from the south. I sit sometimes and wonder if things would have been different if we could re-live our lives and make better choices. Yes, maybe it would turn out differently, but family is all we have through good times and challenging times. With all the imperfections, dysfunctional behaviours and moments of madness. My family has been my rock and a tower of strength. All that I am and all I will ever be, I owe to God above and my family who love me unconditionally.

I have four siblings, three brothers and a sister. My brother Andrew is the one I look up to, although he is younger than I. Omar is the man of silent wisdom well beyond his years. Shanoi, the youngest, is the entrepreneur taking on the world; Marsha, our sister, is the one that keeps us grounded and connected to our roots. Though our parents are not together anymore, they have paved the way for us through many difficulties. One of the most important lessons I have learned from them is that life does not have to be perfect for people to love each other. It took us many years to learn this, but eventually, we did.

My parents were born in an era when people did not talk about or expressed their feelings. I used to wish that they could tell us more about how much they loved us, but I now realise I could not blame them; they were merely products of their upbringing. Despite the things they lacked, I would not give them up for anything because now I know they did the best they could, given the circumstances. Today I stand tall because of my parents, and I am equally proud of all they have achieved so late in their lives. They sacrificed their desires so that their children could live better lives. Family is important!

"Family is the engine that propels us to achieve great things."

In this life, it takes heart to rise above challenges and claim your place among the greats. You can't have a spirit which quickly gives into defeat. You can't surrender to feelings of discouragement because it drains you of the will to persevere. Having heart means having a will of steel that refuses to give up even when the odds are against you. When people are trying to negatively influence your decisions, you must stubbornly refuse to give in. It requires heart to stay above the water, especially when the storm is raging all around.

It's one of the most challenging lessons I have had to learn in my brief life. I have not always had heart, and because of this, I have had to wrestle with many disappointments. I have been guilty of giving up in the past because I was more concerned about what people thought of me and not sticking to the task. I allowed adverse circumstances to get the better of me instead of looking at the valuable lessons right in front of me. I have not always been committed to completing anything because I feared I would fail. I have lost heart many times because I could not see the more significant picture life was painting.

However, there came a time when I had to decide how I wanted to live. My circumstances told me I was a failure, but heart told me something different. Heart said to me I was destined for greatness and to find the resolve to walk into my purpose. I listened to heart and drown out the noise of my circumstances. I realise that heart is the one thing that will keep us rising above every situation, no matter how challenging they are. Heart is like that little train making its way up the steep hill repeating the words "I think I can, I think I can" until belief is the only available option. When in doubt of your purpose in life, listen to your heart.

"Follow your heart even when it is pointing you in the direction that you fear the most. It is usually in that direction, you will find what it takes to unlock your greatness".

No one is ever sure where life's road will take them, but it is a certainty that it leads somewhere. With every struggle I've had to face, I have always been aware that I was to do something extraordinary. I have not always paid attention to life's direction, resulting in a delay in discovering my purpose. I have had to deal with failure and disappointment, but I am thankful for the lessons learned along the way. Though I am destined for greatness, I now know that I must recognise and use the opportunities presented with them. Destiny is not about how well we can predict our lives' outcome, but having the insight to use our different experiences to chart our course. This is what I choose to do.

There are no promises or guarantees, but we can do things to make the journey to greatness smoother. I now realise that though we are designed for greatness, it does not happen automatically. I have had to break habits, change my thought process, and re-evaluate my expectations countless times. I am more convinced that life owes me nothing. Everything I will become and the success I will experience will merit how well I have prepared myself. The truth about destiny is that it happens if we will prepare for its arrival.

Destiny is what you make it, and I plan to make it worthwhile. I will no longer live my life with the regret of what could have been. I will make sure that each day I seize each moment given to me and live like there is no tomorrow. I will not wait for things to happen; I am going to make them happen. There is more to life than just wasting away, hoping that things will change. My destiny is to be the change that I want to see, and it means taking on life without fear.

"If you sit around waiting for destiny to arrive, you will eventually become a comfortable place for failure to take up residence".

I am passionate about many things, but my greatest passion is being able to help change lives. I have found my calling in this area, and I can do it with such ease because I genuinely love what I do. Finding your passion is among the best feelings that any human being could ever experience. When you have found your passion, you will never work a day in your life because what you engage in is like a walk through the park. My passion for helping people reach their full potential is like waking up each day to the sweet sound of music playing as I skip along in the summer breeze. What I do, I do it not for the money, but for the joy of seeing just one person come to realise that they are worth more than they could ever imagine.

The truth is, I have not always been this passionate about anything. I have struggled with feelings of inadequacy, low self-worth, and lack of motivation. There was a time when I did not know what I wanted to do with my life. I thought I would be among the unfortunates of this world floating through life without ever finding aim, purpose, or meaning to life. I remember waking up each day, asking the same question. Why am I here? I never received an answer that satisfied me. This, for me, was a source of frustration, and it led me to make several unwise decisions that caused me much pain and anguish. The lesson I learnt from this is that when a person does not know what they are about, they will settle for anything that comes along.

However, now I am a person of purpose with potential waiting to explode. What makes me passionate about helping people is that I have found my zest for living. I have discovered that if we don't know what we are living for; it is impossible to help anyone else. In turn, we can never help ourselves. My enthusiasm comes from knowing that I am called to live an abundant life through the power of a great God who always has my best interest at heart. I can revel in my enthusiasm for living because I know for a fact that everything I do because of it His will. I desire to serve Him, and that helps me to serve others. I am a child of the King, passionate about life and walking in my purpose.

"The soul cannot find satisfaction until it has fulfilled its passion. Begin every day with a clear picture of how you want it to end. Be passionate about life".

It is a beautiful feeling to discover that you are here for a reason. It may require that you must spend time figuring out things, but it is worth the wait. So it is when I came to understand that there was greatness residing in me. To be great in my earlier years, I thought that I had to be a lawyer, doctor, Rhode scholar, or someone prominent. I never felt like I would be capable of meeting those standards, so I resigned to living an ordinary life. I used to think that greatness was just a dream that only the chosen few would experience. I did not know that greatness was merely a matter of changing my perspective on life and going after what I wanted with enthusiasm and purpose.

I came to know greatness by learning to rise above the noise of negativity. If we are to maximize our potential, we must stop listening to negative pronouncements. For a long time, this was my life. As soon as I was told I could not do something, I believed and refused even to try. I dwelt on what people thought about me and my abilities, and all it did was stifle my growth. It was not until I made the conscious decision to come out of my shell of self-doubt and low self-worth that things changed. Greatness begins in our minds, and I have learnt the secret of freeing my mind and have found a touch of greatness.

My path to discovering my greatness has been nothing short of amazing. I have learned so much about myself and understand that there is so much I still must learn. I am not fearful of the unknown, and I look forward to each challenge that life has to throw at me because I have discovered the power in me. My greatness is not about achievements, nor about gaining material things; it is all about finding my purpose and reaching for the stars. My greatness is what I live for, and I will settle for nothing less than the best of me. I will not give up until I know that I have done all I can to fulfill my destiny, which means finding that touch of greatness.

"Everyone is born with a touch of greatness. We must find a way to ignite that spark and fan the flames until you can't control the fire that burns within you".

"Sticks and stones may break my bones, but words can never hurt me". Whoever came up with that statement did not understand the destruction that hurtful words can have on a person's life. I know firsthand what negative words can do to a person's development. I lived it. For a significant portion of my life, I existed in an environment where hurtful words were thrown like poisonous darts, and it did much damage to my self-esteem. I have had harsh words thrown at me that cut me to the core of my soul. I often thought I would break under their pressure because I am only human.

Negative words can allow people to look at life from a perspective of despair and defeat. They are mainly harmful when they are spewed from the mouths of those who should be in your circle of trust. Sometimes the very people that we depend on to lift us from the depths of defeat are the ones who sink us deeper by the things they say. I dealt with people I expected to push me towards my purpose, which made me feel like nothing because of some inappropriate comment or self-defeating revelation. Words are not just wind; they have the power to create storms that blow so hard they turn into discouragement.

Though words have broken me, I have not fallen to pieces because of the strength of those who spoke life into a wounded soul. If negative words are poisonous, then positive words are the antidote. All the negative words that I have heard cannot be compared to the positive ones that have been a part of my life. Whenever I hear negative words today, I remind myself that whatever anyone has to say about me is not my reality because I am full of purpose. Words will never again break me because the hand of a loving God has proven that I am unbreakable. I need to believe in the power of the one in whose image I was wonderfully created.

"Don't become a slave to the opinions of people who don't have your best interest at heart".

I am a work in progress; I am not where I need to be yet, but I am committed to working hard to getting there. It is not by strength that I do what I do, but God continues to guide me, and to Him, I owe it all. I have been lost, beaten up, used and abused, but I stand tall because I have overcome and found my purpose. However, I am far from perfection because He is still working on me. I have failed, given up and ran away from challenging situations, but His hand keeps pulling me back to the place where I can be useful to Him and others. Even when the path gets dark and I have to feel my way around, I know that He is with me because He is not done yet. He is still working on me!

I'm a diamond in the rough that is being shaped into a crown jewel. I come with all my faults, warts and all; I am that lump of clay without shape until He moulds me into something of purpose. I am confident of what the final product will look like because I know He is still working on me. I am not always patient; sometimes, I run ahead of God and do my own thing. I am thankful that He keeps pulling me back gently, reminding me that He is still working on me.

I don't know where He will lead me eventually, and it's not something I am too concerned about, but what I do know is that I plan to enjoy the journey. I know I will mess up sometimes, so I won't even pretend that I am perfect. My life is not about how many times I have fallen. It is about those times I have risen to claim my place among the greats. I know I can do all things because He is with me every step of the way. There will be many bumps in the road, some hills and valleys, but that's just life. No matter what it takes, I will not give up. After all, He knows who I am and what I can become because He is still working on me.

"We are being moulded by the potter's hand into vessels that are worthy of His praise and honour".

I have taken many directions in my life. Some have led me towards finding my purpose, while others have led me down the path of self-destruction. The most destructive thing that anybody can do to themselves is to have neither aim nor direction in life. For a significant portion of my life, I was that person; I had no leadership, no passion, and not driven to achieve much of anything. Waking up each day was all about going through the motions of working a 9-5 job, hoping to make ends meet at the end of each month. I expected little out of life and did little to change my perception. The most important lesson I learned in all of this is that we will hit nothing whenever we aim at nothing.

Through the remarkable transforming power of God, I have not only found direction, but I have discovered my purpose, and I am passionately pursuing it. It is indeed a great feeling to have figured out the answer to the question "Why I am here"? My reason for being alive is to be an instrument of change to searching souls. I have not always believed that I can do this, but my God reminds me I can do all things through the strength that He provides, and this has become my mantra. Finding direction is not about making my own path. It is going where He sends me with the confidence that He has already set things in motion for my success.

To everyone searching for that pathway that leads to joy and fulfilment, I say to you, keep going at it because the journey will be worth it. Finding direction may require having to struggle with several failures, meet with disappointments, and taste the bitterness of defeat many times. However, the most important thing about finding direction is that the experience gained proves invaluable along the way. Reflecting on my journey, I realise I am wiser because of what I have been through, even with the battle scars. I found direction, but my most valuable treasure is discovering my purpose, which keeps me pressing on towards success.

"Without the storm blowing, we would not know the strength of our sail."

I have found that the most challenging thing I have had to face on my journey to purposeful living is owning my truth. I have tried to live the facade of what the world defines as success and always found it bitterly disappointing. I deceived myself, believing if I had material things or more educational achievements under my belt, it would satisfy me. These things proved to be nothing but an illusion, offering temporary hope and ideas of grandeur. I thought that if I could maintain the spectacle, then somehow I could run with the crowd. I soon realized that if I lied to myself often enough, the risk of believing those lies is multiplied. The only way I could break free from the mirage of a glamorous life is to own my truth.

My truth is who I am; my past circumstances don't make me less than anyone; they only strengthen me. I realise I do an injustice, living a lie to please people in my life. It is not worth giving up the best of me so that I can get the approval of those who consider themselves important. Owning my truth has taught me I am worthy of sitting among the beggars feasting on milk and honey and celebrating with kings and queens at dinner. I own my truth because it is what makes me human. I refuse to hide behind a curtain of embarrassment because my circumstances have not always been the best. My truth is who I am, whom I want to be, and whom I wish to the world to see.

Anyone who reads my story, I say own your truth and don't be afraid of what it says about you. You will only experience real satisfaction when you can be honest with what you have been through. It has taken me many years to learn this valuable lesson, but I am better because of it. My truth no longer scares me. It does not embarrass me, because though it is my truth, it does not control my outlook on a bright future. If you can't handle my truth, my circle is not for you.

"Freedom comes when we allow our hearts to believe the truth about ourselves. Own your truth, even the ugliest details of our lives holds valuable lessons".

When you get to that place in life where you realise the value of simple things, it results in gratitude. This is where I am now. I appreciate life in its purest form and look forward to living it on those terms. This fantastic feeling and passion for living did not spring upon me. It happened because of the many experiences I had to live through. Life does not owe us any favours, and what we get out of it is what we will put into it. For this reason, I refuse to live as a victim. I will stop complaining about all the things I don't have and focus more on appreciating even the simplest things I have.

I take nothing for granted. Life is short, and there is no guarantee of what will happen tomorrow. Today, while I am in control of the simple things, I will make sure that I revel in each moment. I will log on to living as if there is no time left to do anything else; life has a way of teaching valuable lessons when we need it. No matter how many hardships I face, I don't know how to give up, because life has taught me well. The obstacles I have had to overcome make me appreciate I can live out my purpose each day. All I have done, the mistakes made, and the failures have led me to this sense of appreciation for life.

There is no more excellent feeling than living, knowing that you have given your best to the life you have lived. I am not at that place yet, my best is still to come, but I am thankful that I have been privileged to take this journey. There is so much of life to be discovered, and the thought of stepping into the unknown is breathtaking. Yes, there will be some hardships to face, but that will not stop me from celebrating life to the fullest. Appreciating this moment in time is a joy that the world deserves to know, and I will make it my mission to share everything I know.

"The key to abundant living is a desire for living that outweighs your fear of the unknown. To live abundantly, vision must meet purpose, followed up by action".

There is no reason to hold back from what I know to be true. I have come a far way, and now it is time to soar to greatness. I have spent learning through various experiences all the years have been preparing me to fulfil my destiny. I have no time to be timid or to feel threatened by anyone. Life is what each of us makes it out to be, trials and all. There is no reason to hold back, even if there are those present who can't stand the thought of my success. For too long, I have been afraid to step out in faith and take on the challenge of living my best life now. I will not hold back because the price of success is always worth it.

I will take more chances, be bolder, and endeavour to walk confidently in the truth I now know about myself. I am beautifully fashioned in the image of God, who has called me to live an abundant life. I have so much that I still need to accomplish, and there is not much time to get it all done, so I will begin doing them now. I will not waste valuable time dwelling in the past because there is little good that can come from it. I will press on regardless of how my detractors seek to celebrate only my weaknesses. I am active and purpose-driven and refuse to become a victim of circumstances.

I will not hold back; I am pressing on in style; life is too short to play dead. Life owes me nothing, but I am going to take everything I can from it. There is only one chance to do all that I want to do, and I will hold nothing back. A wasted life is no life to live at all. My holding back does nothing to help others unlock their potential and find their purpose. Life is a gift, and there is one opportunity to live it to the fullest, and I will choose to do just that. My life will be lived not just for me, but also for others to unleash the greatness that I know is within them.

"When we hold back, we only succeed in hiding what we were meant to be when God first created us".

I have always been somewhat of a clown. In high school, I was the one to be the life of the party. Whenever a prank was conceived or mischief underway, it was almost a guarantee that I would be somehow involved. I would be the first to have a good laugh at the expense of anyone unfortunate enough to fall prey to a well-timed joke. I would be the one to make a snide comment in the middle of a class, causing disruption that would land me in the principal's office or serving detention after school. I knew how to make light of any situation, no matter how severe. On the surface, I was the classic comedian, and I played the role like a maestro conducting an orchestra.

Sometimes the best way to hide pain is to mask it with something that others find easy to deal with. My fun-loving personality was a defense mechanism for covering my pain. Under the crisp exterior was a soul struggling to comprehend what could have gone so wrong. Why did my parents get divorced? Why did we have to go back to living in a family yard where we were often treated poorly? Why was there not enough money to go to school? So many questions in the life of a child, it was enough to blow the mind. I took the route of turning all this negativity into a comedic affair. It worked well for a while, but it eventually catches up with you, as I was about to learn.

There came a time when I could no longer hide what I was going through, and it started to become destructive. The ability to make light of stressful situations is a gift that can become a curse. Somewhere along the road, my laughter

turned into episodes of anger, my joy would transform into pain, and I was left swimming in a sea of uncertainty. I had to learn that even though a joke could temporarily block the pain, it was not a sufficient remedy.

There is a lot that is going on underneath it, but my story is not finished. The scared, unsure child I was yesterday is growing each day. I still love a good joke and will take every opportunity to construct a good prank, but I will not use these things to mask my pain. The only way to deal with life is to meet it head-on, even its parts that bring distress. We may have to deal with some bumps and bruises, but it will always be better than playing the fool.

"Don't settle for living in the shadows when there is so much of you the world needs to see".

It is a joy watching children grow in their natural environment. There is something very refreshing about their innocence; it puts your soul at ease. It is not a coincidence that Jesus Christ compares entering the Kingdom of Heaven to having little children's nature. Children are gifts to the world in their laughter, conversation and playfulness. I am privileged to be a father to a vibrant son, Timothy-Jordan. The lessons I have learned interacting with and observing him are not taught in any classroom. A valuable lesson I have learnt is that we can love our children unconditionally. This gives us a better understanding of God's unconditional love for humanity. Timothy-Jordan has taught me that love is a choice, and I choose to love him without limits.

Watching Timothy-Jordan at play with his cousins, classmates or friends at church has helped me understand they live in their own little world. Listening to their conversations, stories and arguments have made me realise how much we take for granted. They have their opinions and observations on current affairs. They understand how the world functions and they have the same emotions as adults. Everything that affects us affects them and sometimes as adults, we forget this important detail.

Through observing his interactions with others, I have learnt that children don't know how to hate. Sudden arguments and fights quickly return to wholesome friendships. Think about this for a moment: adults reinforce most of the negative behaviours a child has. A child's natural inclination to anything that disturbs their peace is to get over it and go back to the business of having fun. If they can work through their issues without adult interference most times, they do so, and the results are memorable.

As I watch Tim grow more and more, it's dawning on me that a child's job is not to worry. The only job children have in this world is to be children. They should not be playing adult roles nor taking on responsibilities. It is not in their job description to look after the emotional well-being of adults. All they need to do is focus on being children. We must shoulder the burdens and cares of life while they get to live and enjoy an abundant life. Their time will come when they take over from where we have left off, but until such time, they have a right to be children and we ought to do everything in our power to protect this right.

Abundant living is a life without limits, and my son Timothy-Jordan has taught me the meaning of this. He feels safe and confident that his parents will always be there for him, no matter the odds. He does not worry about what will happen tomorrow because he knows he can depend on his parents to provide the best life. He knows that even if he falls or fails, we will catch him, encourage him, and hold his hand when needed. He has the freedom to pursue the best part of his life to be a child. If you seek to live an abundant life, you probably need to look at the children you have in your life because there is so much we can learn from them. Living through the eyes of a child puts us in a beautiful place to see the glory of God. These are some simple life-changing lessons learnt from my son Timothy-Jordan Blake.

"The innocence of children reveals our anxieties, insecurities and the fact that we have no other choice but to love them unconditionally".

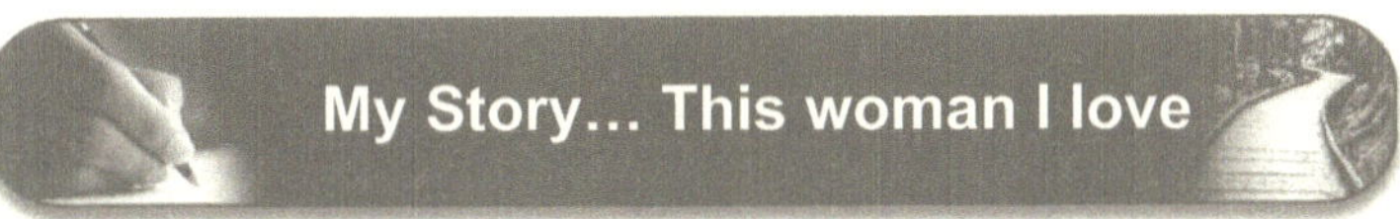

Never in a million years did I think I would find someone who completes me. I was a skeptic in matters of the heart, probably because most of my relationships ended prematurely. However, even a skeptic can become a hopeless romantic if the right person comes along. Racquel and I grew up in Mandeville and went to the same church, but did not consider dating until we were spurred on by Kerry-Ann, her sister. We were friends for a long time and shared many conversations about the people we were dating without expressing interest in each other. However, as fate would have it, nothing can keep them apart when destiny puts people together. Camp 2002 at Ebony Park in Clarendon became the year we would give this dating thing a try, and as they say, the rest is history.

I pay tribute to this woman who makes me want to be a better person every day. Even with all the struggles, the one thing that keeps me committed to her is that I never want to disappoint her. She is the only person to date that can make me sane and insane at the same time. This woman loves unconditionally, and the only requirement is that she is loved in return. She is the epitome of what it means to be a godly woman; she prays for herself to be a good wife and mother.

She prays over our son for him to be a good human being, and she prays for me to be a godly man. When she opens her heart to you, there is no need to fear what will happen next because her soul is made of angels' genuine stuff.

It is great being married to a woman who loves God more than me. I have never had to worry about her compromising her values for anyone. When she speaks, she commands the attention of those around her because she believes in truth. She chooses her words carefully, and when her words hurt, she is quick to make amends. Her remarkable strength comes from her daily indulgence in God's word. She studies to be approved by God, whom she serves with all her being, and her foundation is truth. This woman I love is the perfect example of the virtuous wife, a woman after God's own heart.

Racquel is a gem, and my life is so much better with her in it. She is my partner for life, someone I look forward to growing old with. On this journey called life, few people will get the chance to say they found love, but I will not be one of them. I have been loved many times over, and I am confident that she will love me until the end of her days. This woman I love knows me more than I know myself, and I will do my very best to make her the happiest woman on this side of heaven.

"As we grow old together, we will bask in the memories of a love that does not fade with time."

It is interesting how an event can alter the course of life. In 1998, at one of the lowest points in my life, I obeyed the gospel of Jesus Christ. Since then, my life has not been the same, and I have no regrets. If I had to do it again, I would have decided at an even earlier age. Everything that I am and whom I am becoming, I attribute to God's unwavering love and abundant mercy. I am learning daily to live, love and laugh because His word continues to give me hope in all things. There is no greater joy than knowing that my life is entirely in His hands, and I can trust Him to work out every situation for my benefit (Romans 8: 28).

In Jeremiah 29: 11, I am reminded that the Lord is always thinking of me; therefore, I don't need to fear anything that life throws my way. I have had to battle so many challenges in my brief life; I did not think I would have made it this far. However, because I obeyed Jesus Christ, I am convinced that my battles were a precursor to my victory. I still have days when I must fight hard to stay alive, but now I fight knowing that the battle does not belong to me, but the Lord who fights for me. God did not promise to make everything easy, but He promised to stick around until all is accomplished. I draw comfort from knowing that His will must always be done, no matter what the outcome, and His will is for me to enjoy the best of what He gives.

Like Paul in Philippians 4: 11-13, I have learned how to use my circumstances to bring honour to Jesus Christ, my Lord. In the past, if life was not going the way I wanted, I would resort to destructive behaviours that made things worst. I blamed the world for all my problems and was not willing to alter my perception of life. My relationship with Jesus Christ provides perspective, and that is what I have now. Things that mattered in the past now appear minor details in a life that promises so much more. Now I live my life one day at a time, giving praise to God for even the smallest change that He makes in me. Life is not so much about what the future holds, but more about learning how to appreciate living in the moment; I know this because I have met Christ.

I have no reservations about taking on this new life. I look forward to many more years of sharing my faith with the world. Because I met Christ, I finally understand what is required of me to live a full life. I am confident that the best is yet to come, and I patiently wait for it to happen. I owe it all to Jesus, who is the author and finisher of my faith. I trust Him when he says I have nothing to fear because he continues to prove Himself. Because I met Him, I boldly journey into the unknown and know I will come out with the assurance of His deliverance.

"I can do all things through Christ, who gives me strength."

I believe what makes life worth living is the legacy we leave behind, especially for the benefit of those we love. I want my legacy to be not of fame and fortune, but a story of how I used my gifts to serve humanity. I got caught up focusing on the unimportant stuff as much as the average person, but I know now that these things are not lasting. The stuff that goes into creating a legacy is the things that must stand the test of time and bear much scrutiny. My legacy is more about the people I have served and not about those who helped my selfish interest. I want the world to know that I lived, but I did not just live; I also contributed to making this world better for others to live. I write my story each day knowing that there is the possibility that in the future, someone will need to read it to find their path to greatness. I want to leave behind some useful words that will help someone understand that they also play a role in this thing call life.

My son is my pride and joy, and I want him to know that his father is all that I say I am. Sometimes we are convinced that our children's legacy is the plethora of material things we leave behind. A legacy in fancy cars, expensive houses, bank accounts or Ivy League education, but in how much we have invested in the lives of those we love. I want my son to know that I am a man willing to live and die by principles of fairness, justice and a love for the humanity of others (Micah 6: 8). I want him to understand that positions of power and privilege must not be used to destroy others, but demand greater responsibility from those who wheel them. My legacy to my son is about striving to maintain a balance in life. For every hour of work I've done, I want to give enough time to enjoy living. I don't want to be known as a father who sacrificed his family upon the altar of pursuing success, fame, and fortune.

My legacy is offering the world the best of me. I will make no promise to change the world, but I will commit to improving the small part I occupy. Life is too short not to live it doing something meaningful, and so with the limited time that I have, I am going to live it creating memories. I want to leave behind a legacy that will be etched somewhere in the pages of history, not to be remembered but to help someone find their way to their greatness. My legacy is my story; these words I write are more than letters on paper. They are the words that have shaped me to become a man filled with passion and purpose. One day, whether I am still alive or long departed from this earth, I pray that some man, woman, boy or girl will read these words and begin their journey to abundant living. I write my story, a journey of struggle and perseverance, a legacy that the world deserves to know.

"Our legacy is not found in the abundance of things we leave behind. Our legacy is the story we write daily by the lives we live so that others will have an example to follow."

Home is where the heart is……. this seems to be a cliché, but it is one that holds much meaning for me. As you would have read previously, I grew up moving around a lot, which left me with an aversion to change. When I got married, one of the first things I told my wife Racquel is that we needed to buy a house. I didn't particularly like moving because I moved a lot in my younger years. God blessed us with the opportunity to purchase our house in the second year of our marriage. This house has helped to form a part of what I call home. It is not the house that makes the home, but it is in the house where the home dwells. The people who exist within the structure, the activities carried out, and the memories made that qualify a house to be called a home. When I speak of home, I refer to the above things and so much more.

Anyone that knows me well knows I am completely in love with the idea of having a home. I love thinking about home, and I enjoy going home. There is something extraordinary about home. My home is my go-to place, my haven, my castle, the place where I feel comfortable being me. It's the place where the people I hold dearest to my heart see the best and worst of me. Home is where family share moments of joy, periods of sorrow, celebrations of success, and triumph over obstacles. It's that place where we find the courage to love without limits. Home is where the heart is; it brings a feeling that cannot be traded for all the treasures of the earth. No matter where I go in this world, I am always anticipating the time when I can finally come home.

I don't expect everyone to fully understand my idea of home because you will have to live it to appreciate it. Home is not just a concept; it is what the heart longs for, and the only thing that will satisfy the soul. Every human being deserves the experience of having a home; it is not a privilege, it is a right. Home is my place of escape, a place where I don't worry about the troubles of the world. When I come home, I am anticipating the comfort of a sacred space where nothing else matters.

"A man's home is where his heart resides.
The place where he has the freedom
to be the best of himself".

There are challenges throughout life; facing them is what makes the difference between failure and success. I know this because it has been the story of my life. Even when I have conquered one mountain, there is another one waiting in the distance. Sometimes when I fall, I am hard on myself because I somehow convince myself that I should have known better because of past experiences. At other times I am doing well, and I forget my celebration is only for the moment. I take nothing for granted because life is short and challenging times lie ahead. The thing that remains constant is that despite what happens, the desire to overcome obstacles is what keeps me going.

I have realized that if I am going to defeat the obstacles set before me, I must first understand that nobody owes me anything. It is nobody's job to fuel my success. Whatever help I am given along the way comes from living in preparation mode. If life gets the chance, it will place every obstacle in our path to keep us defeated, but I have learnt that life did not choose me to be defeated. Life beats those who want to remain unaware that we are not that special for it to single us out. I am growing up to understand that if I work hard and consistently, I will eventually receive what is due to me. I am an overcomer because even when I feel defeated, I can accept it for what it is.

The day that a bird stops flying is the day it stops having a reason to live. If I continue to allow my failures to keep me subdued, I have no reason to wake up each day. So, I choose to overcome because there is nothing in life that has the power to make me its victim. I can do all things through Christ who gives me strength is what I choose to live by each day. These are not just words that have been strung together for good measure. They are words that remind every child of God that this is His desire for us. I am not here on earth to be a failure; I was born to move mountains.

People have failed me, and I have failed people. I have failed at jobs; I have stopped dreaming; I have failed at pursuing my passion. I have wanted to give up many times, but there is something in me that makes me refuse to give up because I know I must overcome. There are no more excuses to be made because they are of little value to me or anyone else. If I am going to overcome, I need to set sail even when I am uncertain of the wind's direction because I know who controls the wind. I can overcome, I will overcome, and I overcome because it is my destiny.

"Never give up, even when it seems the odds are against you. Your breakthrough is a sure thing"!

These words I have written are a glimpse into my life. They remind me and anyone who reads them that the journey to finding passion and purpose is never finished. With everything that I have accomplished, I wake each day conscious that there is much more to be discovered on this journey. My story will continue to unfold as long as life remains in this mortal body. Somebody still needs to read my words and know that whatever they have dreamed about can be their reality. This story is not finished because there is a voice in my head telling me that there are still many more miles to go. Somebody out there needs to read these words and understand that nothing in this life is impossible if we dare to believe. It isn't over because I am still breathing, and my life is a constant reminder that the best is yet to come.

As I write these words, I realise I have conquered some significant hurdles, but I am far from satisfaction. My insecurities are a thing of the past, and now I am a power-packed man on a mission. My goal is to unlock the door to my abundant life and share from the fountain of truth. I desire to wake up each day with the confidence and determination that I can accomplish great things. I want to sleep at nights, knowing that there is nothing I would regret not doing if it were my last day. I approach everyday living life intentionally; I refuse to be a victim of circumstances because God has given me the gift of insight and wisdom and the power of a sound mind.

Nothing last forever, time is unpredictable, so while time is on my side, I will do all I can to leave a mark on this world. I will leave no stone unturned until I have squeezed every inch out of living passionately and purposefully. I will tell my story as many times as it takes until someone realise they are meant to soar like eagles. No one knows when time will turn into eternity, so while time is on my side; I will not only write my story but will live it with all I have in me. This story I am writing is important. I will not be distracted or listen to the voices of detractors. Their part in my story is a reminder that my destiny still awaits me, even when no one believes in me. It isn't over; a few chapters are yet to be written.

"Where there is hope, nothing is ever final. Hope will keep us fighting until our mission to live an abundant life is complete".

Paul A. Blake is a vibrant and dynamic keynote speaker trained at the University of the West Indies, United Theological College, St. Michael's Theological College and the Jamaica School of Preaching and Biblical Studies. He believes in the power of decisive thinking in effecting change in the lives of all persons who have a desire to live an abundant life. He is a vibrant Jamaican man who has defied the odds and wants to share his incredible story of finding passion and purpose with the world.

Paul is CEO and Founder of Words Worthit Motivational Speaking and Training Co. Ltd. This faith-based company specializes in helping people reach their heights of success through purposeful living. He believes if people can change the way they think, they can maximize their potential and be passionate about life. Paul's story is one of resolve, strength, and passion shared locally and internationally on radio and television. He is frequently involved in giving motivational presentations and engaging in workshops at several organizations including companies, schools and other tertiary institutions.

He currently serves at the Old Harbour Church of Christ, preaching and teaching. He is a Licensed Marriage Officer and Counsellor and the author of the motivational series Words to Inspire Volumes 1 & 2 and 40 Days to Abundant Living.

Paul is married to Racquel since May 2007. The union has produced one extraordinary son, Timothy-Jordan. Paul's mantra is "I can do all things through Christ."

Please contact Paul at paulblake@wordstoinspireja.com or visit the website www.wordstoinspireja.com to check our services and offerings for coaching, speaking, and seminar inquiries.

Connect with Paul:
Instagram: @wordstoinspire
Twitter: @wordsworthitjam
Facebook@ Words to Inspire
LinkedIn: @ www.linkedin.com/in/paul-blake-926a8089

Other Books by
Paul A. Blake

• Lessons From a Father to His Son
• Words to Inspire Volume one
• Words to Inspire Volume two
• 40 Days to Abundant Living
• Abundant Living E-book